ASTROLOGY

GEMINI

BY ABBY DOTY

WWW.APEXEDITIONS.COM

Apex is distributed by North Star Editions:
sales@northstareditions.com | 888-417-0195

Produced for Apex by Red Line Editorial.

Photographs ©: Shutterstock Images, cover (illustration, constellation), cover (background), 1, 4–5, 10–11, 12, 13, 14–15, 16–17, 18, 19, 20–21, 22–23, 25, 26, 27, 29; iStockphoto, 6, 7, 8, 9

Library of Congress Control Number: 2025939151

ISBN
979-8-89250-784-4 (hardcover)
979-8-89250-813-1 (paperback)
979-8-89250-870-4 (ebook pdf)
979-8-89250-842-1 (hosted ebook)

Printed in the United States of America
Mankato, MN
012026

NOTE TO PARENTS AND EDUCATORS

Apex books are designed to build literacy skills in striving readers. Exciting, high-interest content attracts and holds readers' attention. The text is carefully leveled to allow students to achieve success quickly. Additional features, such as bolded glossary words for difficult terms, help build comprehension.

TABLE OF CONTENTS

CHAPTER 1

THE TWINS

Gemini is a **constellation**. Its name means "the twins" in Latin. Some people say it looks like two bodies.

The stars that make up Gemini look like two stick figures holding hands.

Bright stars represent the two heads. These stars are called Castor and Pollux. The names come from a Greek **myth**. It tells of two brothers.

Castor and Pollux appear in several Greek myths. They were said to be skilled fighters.

FAST FACT

Castor is actually a group of six stars. But to people's eyes, they look like one star.

The star Pollux (left) is a bit brighter than Castor. Pollux also has a more orange color.

According to myths, Castor and Pollux were very close. Zeus helped them stay together forever.

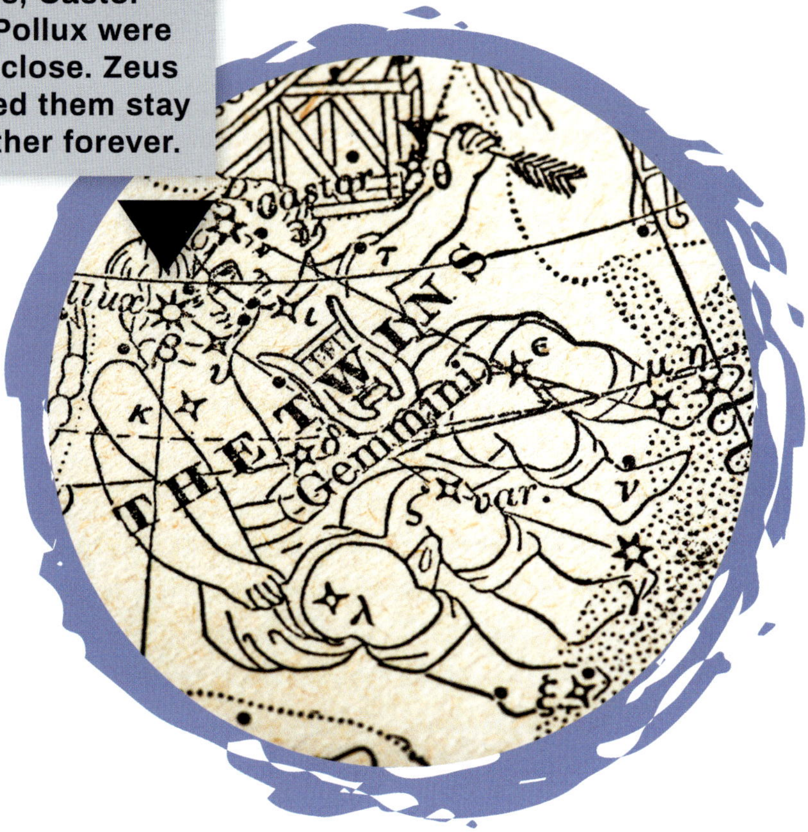

In the myth, Castor dies in battle. So, Pollux goes to the god Zeus. He asks Zeus for help. Zeus places the brothers in the sky as stars.

MORE STORIES

In Egypt, people said the stars formed a pair of goats. Arabian stories said they were two peacocks. Others said they were Romulus and Remus. A myth said those twins founded Rome.

One Roman myth said that Romulus and Remus were raised by a wolf.

CHAPTER 2

SIGNS AND SEASONS

Gemini is one of the 12 **zodiac** signs. Each sign is based on a different constellation. And each is matched with part of the year.

The 12 zodiac signs are based on old ideas about how stars and planets move through space.

A person's sun sign is their main sign. It's based on their birth date and said to shape the core of who they are.

Gemini is the third sign. Its time begins around May 21. It ends around June 21. People born during this time have Gemini as their sun sign.

FAST FACT

Each person also has a moon sign. It's based on the moon's location when they were born.

Moon signs are said to reveal people's inner thoughts and feelings.

Geminis often like going out and having adventures.

Astrology claims that signs shape how people think and act. For example, Geminis are said to be **curious** and playful.

SUN SEASONS

During each sign's season, all people may take on that sign's traits. Gemini's time is said to inspire change. People may get new ideas. Or they may have fun trying new things.

CHAPTER 3

ABOUT GEMINI

Each zodiac sign is matched with one of four **elements**. Gemini is an air sign. Air signs are said to have lots of ideas and energy.

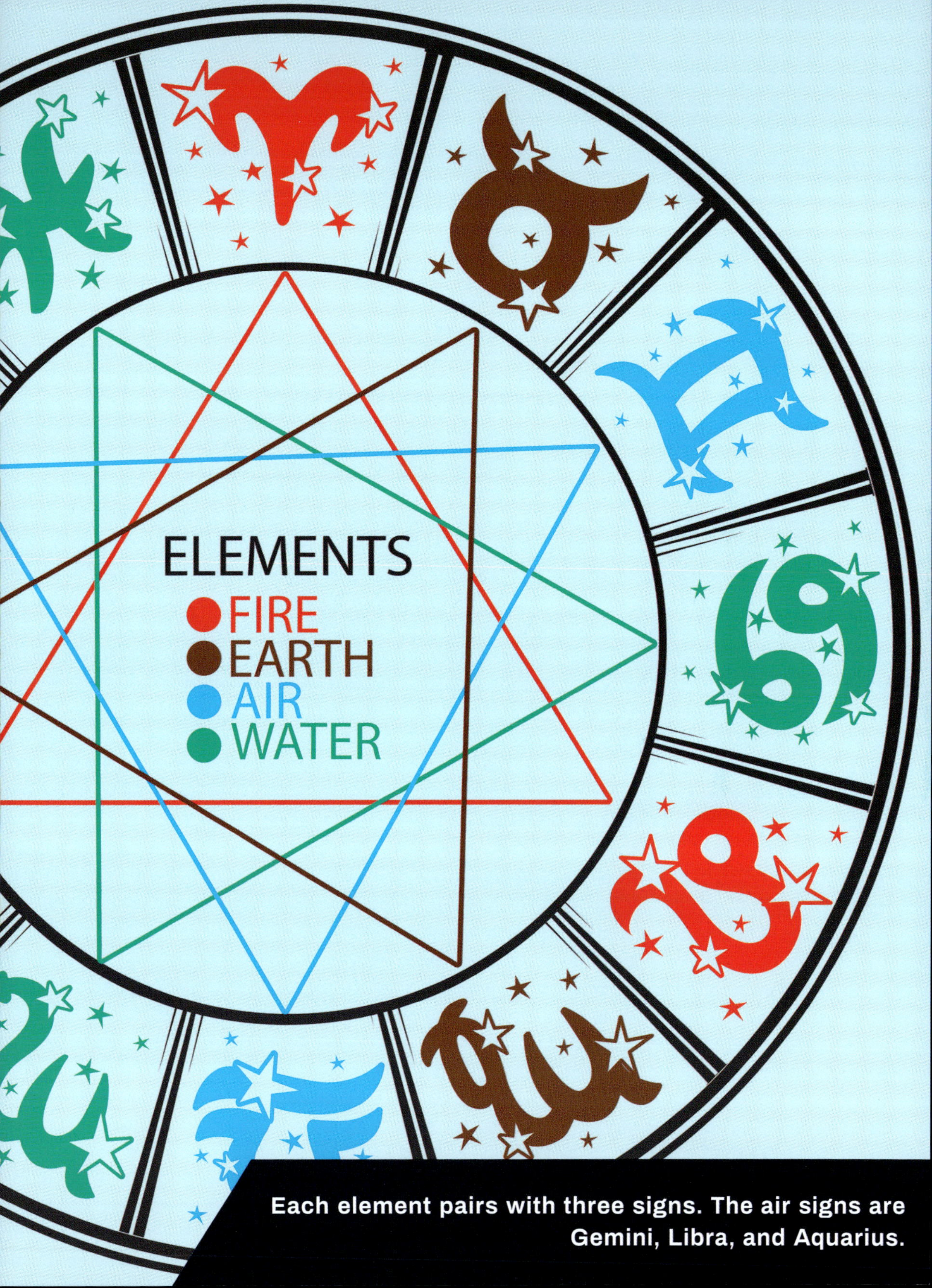

Each element pairs with three signs. The air signs are Gemini, Libra, and Aquarius.

Gemini's ruling planet is Mercury. Ruling planets are said to shape how people act. Mercury is linked to communicating. And Geminis often love talking and being with others.

In Roman myths, Mercury often brought messages to and from other gods.

Mercury is the fastest planet in the solar system. It travels nearly 29 miles per second (47 km/s).

FAST FACT

Mercury is a fast-moving planet. Geminis are also known for thinking and acting quickly.

Each sign also has a **glyph**. Gemini's looks like a Roman numeral two. It represents twins.

The glyph helps show that a Gemini can have two different sides to how they act.

DOUBLE TROUBLE

Geminis may change how they act based on who they are around. As a result, people sometimes call them two-faced. But many Geminis aren't being dishonest. They are just good at **adapting**.

CHAPTER 4

STAYING BUSY

In astrology, Geminis are known for being social. They often have many friends. And they can get along with many different types of people.

Geminis tend to connect well with others. They also love having fun.

Geminis also like to stay busy. They often have many interests and hobbies. They enjoy being creative and trying new things.

FAST FACT

Famous Geminis include Kendrick Lamar, Tom Holland, and Venus Williams.

Many Geminis love to travel and visit new places.

Sometimes, Geminis have trouble focusing. They may jump from one project to the next. But they can build good habits. For example, they can finish one project before starting another.

Geminis may switch quickly from one hobby to another. They like to learn a little bit about many things.

Geminis often love writing. They may also be good at explaining things to others.

GEMINI JOBS

Geminis often enjoy jobs that involve learning new things. Some become teachers. Others work as journalists. They write and **report** on many topics.

COMPREHENSION QUESTIONS

Write your answers on a separate piece of paper.

1. Write a few sentences explaining the main ideas of Chapter 4.
2. Do you like to try lots of new things? Or would you rather stick with things you already know?
3. What does *Gemini* mean in Latin?
   - A. twins
   - B. goats
   - C. peacocks
4. According to astrology, what might a Gemini enjoy the most?
   - A. staying home and being alone
   - B. doing the same task over and over
   - C. going to a party with lots of people

5. What does **communicating** mean in this book?

*Mercury is linked to **communicating**. And Geminis often love talking and being with others.*

A. sharing messages or ideas
B. ignoring people's messages
C. staying away from people

6. What does **focusing** mean in this book?

*Sometimes, Geminis have trouble **focusing**. They may jump from one project to the next.*

A. having lots of different hobbies
B. paying attention to one thing
C. making friends with new people

Answer key on page 32.

GLOSSARY

adapting
Changing to fit a particular situation.

constellation
A group of stars that form a shape.

curious
Liking to find out new things.

elements
The four forces (air, earth, fire, and water) that zodiac signs are matched with and said to be shaped by.

glyph
A shape that stands for a word or idea.

myth
A well-known story from the past that often includes magic.

report
To tell others about an event or idea, usually by speaking or writing.

zodiac
The set of 12 signs used in astrology, based on a part of the sky that the sun appears to move through each year.

TO LEARN MORE

BOOKS

Goldstein, Margaret J. *Mysteries of Stars*. Lerner Publications, 2021.

Loh-Hagan, Virginia. *Star Signs*. Cherry Lake Publishing, 2021.

Milroy, Liz. *Explore Mercury*. Lerner Publications, 2021.

ONLINE RESOURCES

Visit **www.apexeditions.com** to find links and resources related to this title.

ABOUT THE AUTHOR

Abby Doty is a writer, editor, and booklover from Minnesota. Her sun sign is Aquarius.

INDEX

ANSWER KEY:
1. Answers will vary; 2. Answers will vary; 3. A; 4. C; 5. A; 6. B